GOOGLE MOTOROLA EDGE 50 FUSION USER GUIDE

Comprehensive and Detailed Guide to Mastering the Motorola Edge 50 Fusion for Beginners

By

Robert P. Mendez

Intentionally left blank

All rights reserved. No part of this publication may be reproduced, distributed, or transmitted in any form or by any means, including photocopying, recording, or other electronic or mechanical methods without the prior written permission of the copyright owner, except in the case of brief quotations embodied in critical reviews and certain other non commercial use permitted by copyright law.

Copyright © Robert P. Mendez, 2024

Table of contents

INTRODUCTION.. 9
CHAPTER 1... 15
Welcome to the Motorola Edge 50 Fusion............... 15
    Introducing the Motorola Edge 50 Fusion............... 16
    A Seamless User Experience with Android............ 19
CHAPTER 2... 27
Getting Started with Your Motorola Edge 50 Fusion... 27
    Powering Up for the First Time................................ 27
    Navigating the Home Screen and Beyond.............33
    Understanding the Notification Panel:.................... 37
CHAPTER 3... 40
Unveiling the Hardware of Your Motorola Edge 50 Fusion.. 40
    A Tour of Your Phone's Layout................................ 40
    Unlocking the Power of Security: Fingerprint Sensor and Options... 48
CHAPTER 4... 52
Unveiling the Software of Your Motorola Edge 50 Fusion.. 52
    Understanding the Android Ecosystem................... 53
CHAPTER 5... 64

Connecting with the World: Making Calls and Texting.. **64**

    Placing and Receiving Calls: The Essence of Communication..64

CHAPTER 6... **74**

Capturing Memories: The Power of the Motorola Edge 50 Fusion Camera......................................**74**

CHAPTER 7... **85**

Unveiling the World Wide Web................................**85**

    Connecting to Wi-Fi Networks: Your Gateway to the Web.. 86

    Exploring the Web with Chrome: Your Window to the World... 90

CHAPTER 8... **96**

Unleashing Entertainment: Music, Videos, Games, and More..**96**

    Unleashing the Power of Streaming Services...... 101

    Expanding Your Productivity Toolkit: Exploring Additional Apps.. 111

CHAPTER 9..**116**

Safeguarding Your Sanctuary................................**116**

    Installing Security Updates: Maintaining a Secure System... 122

CHAPTER 10.. **127**

Advanced Features and Tips for Mastering Your Motorola Edge 50 Fusion..**127**

    Capturing the Moment: Screenshots and Screen Recordings..130

    Enhancing Accessibility: Built-in Features for Everyone...133

Capturing Stunning Photos: Advanced Camera
Settings.. 142
CONCLUSION..148
A Recap of Your Powerful Companion: Key Features
and Benefits... 149
APPENDIX.. 156

Intentionally left blank

INTRODUCTION

Welcome to the Unbound World of Your Motorola Edge 50 Fusion: A Beginner's Guide to Mastering Your Smartphone

Congratulations on getting the elegant and powerful Motorola Edge 50 Fusion! This smartphone offers a realm of possibilities, from seamless communication and immersive entertainment to better productivity and creative discovery. Whether you're a seasoned smartphone user or an inquisitive newbie, this thorough guide is here to enable you to explore the amazing features and functions of your Motorola Edge 50 Fusion.

A Roadmap for Beginners

This user guide is precisely prepared for novices, delivering a straightforward and succinct approach to learning your phone. We realise that managing a new smartphone might be intimidating. Fear not! This tutorial is meant to be your friendly companion, breaking down complicated features into easy-to-understand stages with clear pictures and practical examples.

Unlocking the Essentials

We'll begin by demystifying the essentials. You'll learn how to set up your phone, connect to Wi-Fi networks, make calls and send messages, navigate the simple interface, and customise your home screen with widgets and wallpapers. We'll go further into vital applications like the camera, calendar, and contacts app, ensuring you're comfortable completing routine activities with confidence.

Beyond the Basics: Unveiling Hidden Gems

Once you've understood the core concepts, this tutorial will expose the hidden jewels of your Motorola Edge 50 Fusion. We'll examine special Motorola capabilities (if available on your model), allowing you to exploit gesture-based shortcuts, engage the Active Display for a glance at alerts, or tailor fast launch choices for easy access to your favorite applications.

Empowering Your Photography Passion:

For photography aficionados, we'll expose the secrets behind the amazing camera system. You'll learn how to navigate multiple shooting modes, explore with sophisticated camera settings like exposure control and white balance, and find innovative approaches to take great images and movies.

Transforming Your Productivity:

This guide isn't only about entertainment. We'll provide you with the knowledge to make your Motorola Edge 50 Fusion into a productivity powerhouse. You'll learn how to manage your schedule using the calendar app, make to-do lists to keep organized, and discover a huge library of productivity applications available on the Google Play Store to optimise your workflow.

Troubleshooting with Confidence:

Even the most tech-savvy individuals suffer occasional difficulties. This guide won't leave you stranded. We'll share troubleshooting techniques for common difficulties like battery loss, Wi-Fi connection problems, or app failures. You'll learn how to identify probable causes and execute remedies to keep your phone working well.

A Journey of Continuous Learning:

Technology is a dynamic landscape. This handbook serves as a platform for your further investigation. We'll provide you with essential resources like user manuals, online support websites, forums, and YouTube lessons to keep you current on the newest software upgrades, features, and learning opportunities.

Embrace the Possibilities:

This book is more than simply a user handbook. It's an invitation to explore a world of unlimited possibilities. With the information you'll learn here, you'll convert your Motorola Edge 50 Fusion from a basic gadget into a powerful tool for communication, entertainment, productivity, and creativity. Embrace the trip, explore with new functions, and configure your phone to exactly fit your requirements.

This detailed guide is the key to unlocking the full potential of your Motorola Edge 50 Fusion. So, begin on this amazing voyage, and let's alter your smartphone experience!

CHAPTER 1

Welcome to the Motorola Edge 50 Fusion

Congratulations on getting the Motorola Edge 50 Fusion! This user guide is meant to be your thorough companion while you discover the amazing features and functions of your new smartphone. Whether you're a total rookie stepping into the world of smartphones or just wanting to refresh your expertise on a new device, this guide will provide you with the required steps and insights to master your Motorola Edge 50 Fusion.

Introducing the Motorola Edge 50 Fusion

The Motorola Edge 50 Fusion offers a great balance of design and performance. Its elegant design, boasting a brilliant color palette and an ultra-thin contoured shape, provides a great first impression. But beauty extends beyond appearances. The Edge 50 Fusion has a strong CPU that easily performs ordinary chores and even demanding apps.

Unveiling a Powerhouse Within

The core of the Edge 50 Fusion resides in its powerful CPU. While the actual specs may vary based on your area, you can anticipate a CPU capable of providing smooth and efficient performance. Whether you're surfing the web, multitasking between applications, or playing graphics-intensive games, the CPU offers a lag-free user experience.

Capture Stunning Memories with a Cutting-Edge Camera System

The Edge 50 Fusion lets you record life's moments in amazing detail. The primary camera, equipped with a megapixel sensor (precise megapixel count may vary), gives superb picture quality. Whether you're shooting in brilliant sunshine or capturing low-light scenarios, the camera's sophisticated technology delivers clean and clear photographs. Don't forget about the front-facing camera, great for snapping selfies and participating in video chats.

Immerse Yourself in a Vibrant Display

The Edge 50 Fusion has a dazzling display that brings your visual experiences to life.

The huge screen size, paired with great quality, enables you to watch movies, games, and other material in amazing detail. The display technology, whether OLED or IPS LCD (depending on your exact model), gives brilliant colors, clear images, and good viewing angles. Additionally, the high refresh rate (precise refresh rate may vary) offers seamless browsing and a visually pleasant user experience.

Long-Lasting Power to Keep You Going

Never worry about running out of energy with the Edge 50 Fusion's long-lasting battery. The large capacity battery gives adequate juice to keep you connected throughout the day, even with intensive use. And when you do need to recharge, the fast-charging technology enables you to be back up and running in a short period of time (precise charging speed may vary depending on the model and adapter).

A Seamless User Experience with Android

The Edge 50 Fusion relies on the Android operating system, a familiar and user-friendly platform for many smartphone users. Android provides a vast selection of features and capabilities, enabling you to personalise your phone to match your requirements. From downloading applications and games to managing your contacts and calendar, Android delivers a complete and straightforward user experience.

What's in the Box?

Unboxing your fresh new Motorola Edge 50 Fusion is a wonderful occasion. Let's look into the fundamentals you'll discover within the packaging:

The Motorola Edge 50 Fusion Smartphone: The star of the show, pre-installed with the Android operating system and ready to be explored.

Charging Cable: This cable connects your phone to a power adapter for charging the battery.

Power Adapter: Plugged into a wall socket, the power adapter supplies the required electricity to charge your phone using the provided cable.

SIM Card Ejector Tool: This little tool enables you to securely remove the SIM card tray from your phone. The SIM card is needed for connecting to your mobile network provider.

Quick Start Guide: This brochure gives a quick explanation of the phone's fundamental features and first setup procedure.

Warranty Information: This paper covers the warranty coverage for your phone, ensuring you're aware about your rights and support choices.

Additional Items (May Vary Depending on Region):

In certain locations, your packing could contain extra accessories:

 Protective Case: A pre-installed or included case secures your phone from scratches and mild bumps.
 Wired earbuds: These earbuds enable you to listen to music, make calls, and consume multimedia material.
 Screen Protector: This thin coating protects the phone's display from scratches and fingerprints.

We suggest thoroughly verifying the contents of your package to confirm you have gotten all the listed products. If anything seems missing or damaged, please contact your shop or Motorola support for help.

This chapter has offered a look into the incredible capabilities of the Motorola Edge 50 Fusion. As you go further into the next chapters, you'll obtain a full grasp of the phone's features, capabilities ...and how to manage them with ease. Here's a deeper look at some of the important features you'll encounter:

 A Triple Camera System (or More): While the specific arrangement may vary based on your model, the Edge 50 Fusion has a configurable camera system. The primary high-resolution camera captures superb detail in your images, while other lenses like an ultrawide sensor or a telephoto lens give creative alternatives. You could also discover a depth sensor for better portrait photography.

Artificial Intelligence (AI) Camera Enhancements: The Edge 50 Fusion employs AI capabilities to enrich your photographic experience. Scene recognition intelligently changes camera settings for best results depending on the situation you're taking, while features like HDR (High Dynamic Range) assure balanced exposure in tough lighting circumstances.

Long-lasting Battery with Fast Charging: Equipped with a high-capacity battery, the Edge 50 Fusion delivers prolonged use time on a single charge. Whether you're streaming movies, surfing the web, or playing games, you can count on your phone to keep up. When it's time to recharge, the fast-charging technology lets you to go back to using your phone quickly. (Please note, the precise charging speed may vary based on the model and adapter used.)

Storage Options to Suit Your Needs: The Edge 50 Fusion comes with internal storage to host your applications, photographs, videos, and other stuff. The precise storage capacity may vary based on the selected model. If you desire more room for a big media collection, you may take advantage of the expandable storage option using a microSD card (available separately).

A Sleek and Stylish Design: The Edge 50 Fusion is made to turn attention. Its sleek form and smooth finish give a feeling of refinement, while the bright color choices enable you to express your particular style. The phone is pleasant to carry and operate, making it a suitable companion for daily chores.

A Secure and Customizable User Experience: The Edge 50 Fusion focuses your privacy and security. You may pick from numerous lock screen methods, like fingerprint recognition or face recognition (depending on your model), to secure your data. Additionally, the Android operating system allows for substantial customization, enabling you to modify your phone's layout, themes, and notification settings to create an experience that best meets your tastes.

Built-in Entertainment Features: The Edge 50 Fusion keeps you engaged wherever you go. The high-resolution display and immersive audio experience make it great for viewing movies, programmes, and playing games. The phone also comes pre-installed with entertainment applications and services, letting you to access your favorite material with ease.

We've merely scratched the surface of the Motorola Edge 50 Fusion's possibilities. The next chapters will go further into each of these features and functions, arming you with the knowledge and skills to become a master of your new gadget. Get ready to uncover the full power of the Motorola Edge 50 Fusion and start on a voyage of discovery, connection, and unlimited possibilities.

CHAPTER 2

Getting Started with Your Motorola Edge 50 Fusion

Congratulations for taking the first step towards learning your new Motorola Edge 50 Fusion! This chapter will lead you through the initial setup process, ensuring your phone is ready to use and configured to your preferences.

Powering Up for the First Time

1. Locate the Power Button: The power button is normally positioned on the right side of your phone. It can be a slightly elevated button with a power symbol.

2. Press and Hold the Power Button: With the phone facing you, press and hold the power button for a few seconds. The screen will light, showing the Motorola logo. This shows the phone is starting up.

3. Welcome displays: After the first startup phase, you'll be welcomed by a succession of welcome displays. These windows help you through choosing your desired language, connecting to a Wi-Fi network, and setting up your Google account.

4. Connecting to Wi-Fi: Choose a Wi-Fi network from the available choices. If the network is password-protected, you'll be requested to enter the password. A solid Wi-Fi connection is vital for downloading applications, updating the software, and accessing internet services.

5. Setting Up Your Google Account: A Google account is needed for utilising many of the features on your Android phone. If

you already have a Google account, enter your login details. If you're new to Google accounts, you may create one during the setup process.

6. Date and Time: Ensure your phone shows the right date and time. You may generally opt to configure it automatically depending on your Wi-Fi connection or manually alter the settings.

7. Terms & Conditions: Review and agree to the terms and conditions for using the phone and Google services.

8. more Setup choices: Depending on your model and preferences, you could find more setup choices, such as enabling fingerprint or face recognition for unlocking the phone, restoring data from a backup (covered later in this chapter), and activating Google Assistant.

Installing the SIM Card and microSD Card (if applicable)

1. Locate the SIM Card Tray: The SIM card tray is normally situated on the side of the phone or could be concealed behind a thin cover. Consult your quick start guide or the phone's handbook for the precise position for your individual model.

2. Eject the SIM Card Tray: Use the included SIM card ejector tool (a little pin-like item) to gently push into the allocated hole beside the SIM card tray. The tray should pop out somewhat.

3. Insert the SIM Card: The SIM card normally has a little notch cut out of one corner. Identify the right orientation of the SIM card by aligning the notch with the cutout on the tray. Carefully slide the SIM card into the relevant slot on the tray, ensuring the gold contacts face downwards.

4. slide the microSD Card (Optional): If your phone supports expandable storage via a microSD card, you may slide it into the appropriate slot on the SIM card tray. Refer to your user manual or the marks on the tray to locate the suitable slot. Similar to the SIM card, verify the microSD card is put in the right orientation.

5. Reinsert the SIM Card Tray: Carefully press the SIM card tray back into the phone until it snaps into place.

Transferring Data from Your Old Phone (Optional)

If you're migrating from another smartphone, you may transfer your data to your new Edge 50 Fusion to shorten the setup procedure. Here are two popular methods:

   Using a Google Account: If you used a Google account on your previous phone, you can recover your contacts, calendar events, and certain app data during the initial setup process on the Edge 50 Fusion.

Using a Transfer Cable or App (May Vary Depending on Brand): Some phone manufacturers provide specialised applications or transfer cables to simplify data movement across their devices. Check whether your prior phone's brand gives such an option. Alternatively, there are third-party programmes available that may assist move data across various phone brands.

Navigating the Home Screen and Beyond

Now that your Motorola Edge 50 Fusion is up and running, let's examine the user interface and basic navigation. The home screen is your major hub for accessing all the features and functionality of your phone. It often shows programme icons, widgets (miniature apps that allow rapid access to information or functionality), and a search bar.

Understanding the Home Screen:

 App Icons: These coloured squares or icons indicate the applications loaded on your phone. Tapping an icon starts the related app.
 Widgets: These give easy methods to see information or conduct tasks without launching a complete app. Examples include weather widgets, calendar widgets, and music player widgets. Long-press on an

empty region of the home screen to enter the widget selection menu.

Dock: The dock is normally situated at the bottom of the home screen and may house a few commonly used app icons for easy access.

Search Bar: Use the search bar to easily locate installed applications or search the web using Google.

Swiping Magic:

Mastering gestures is crucial to managing your phone effectively. Here are some crucial swipes to remember:

Swiping Up: Swiping upwards from the bottom of the home screen opens the app drawer, which shows a list of all your installed applications.

Swiping Left or Right: By default, swiping left or right across the home screen navigates between various home screen pages. You may modify the amount of home screen pages afterward.

Swiping Down: Swiping down from the top of the screen exposes the notification panel. This panel shows alerts and notifications from applications, as well as fast settings for regularly used functionalities like Wi-Fi, Bluetooth, and brightness.

Customizing Your Home Screen:

The brilliance of Android rests in its customisation capabilities. You may modify your home screen to suit your tastes. Here's how:

Rearranging App Icons: Long-press on an app icon and then drag it to a new spot on the home screen. You may also transfer them to various home screen pages by swiping left or right while holding the symbol.

Adding Widgets: Long-press on an empty region of the home screen to enter the widget selection menu. Choose the appropriate widget and drag it to a convenient spot on the home screen.

Changing Wallpaper: Long-press on an empty space of the home screen and pick "Wallpaper" from the menu. You may pick from pre-loaded backgrounds or choose a new picture from your collection.

The App Drawer:

The app drawer holds all the programmes loaded on your phone. Here's how to access and browse it:

Swipe Up: As indicated previously, sliding upwards from the bottom of the home screen opens the app drawer.

Searching for applications: Use the search box at the top of the app drawer to quickly discover installed applications by name.

Sorting applications: Most Android phones enable you to arrange applications

36

alphabetically, by most frequently used, or by custom categories.

Understanding the Notification Panel:

The notification panel keeps you informed about crucial notifications and app updates. Here's how to access and manage it:

 Swiping Down: Swipe down from the top of the screen to see the notification panel. This panel shows alerts in a chronological sequence.
 Clearing Notifications: Tap the "X" button in the corner of each notification to clear it separately. You may also slide the notice to the left or right to dismiss it.
   fast Settings: The top area of the notification panel commonly holds fast settings icons for Wi-Fi, Bluetooth, flashlight, and other frequently used services. Tap an icon to turn its status on or

off. You may expand this area by swiping down twice to display more fast settings choices.

Powering Down Your Phone:

When you're done using your phone, you may shut it down to preserve battery life. Here's how:

1. Press and Hold the Power Button: Locate the power button and press and hold it for a few seconds.
2. Power Menu: A power menu will show on the screen.
3. Select "Power Off" or "Shut Down": Choose the option to shut off your phone fully.

By familiarizing yourself with these fundamental navigation strategies, you'll be well on your way to mastering your Motorola Edge 50 Fusion. The next chapters will go further into certain features, permitting you to discover the full potential of your new gadget.

Congratulations!

You've successfully switched on your Motorola Edge 50 Fusion, inserted the SIM card and microSD card (if applicable), and investigated data transfer options. The next chapters will dig further into the features of your new phone, helping you to unleash its full potential.

CHAPTER 3

Unveiling the Hardware of Your Motorola Edge 50 Fusion

The Motorola Edge 50 Fusion sports a sleek and utilitarian design that packs a punch in terms of functions. This chapter gives you a complete grasp of your phone's physical components and their functionality.

A Tour of Your Phone's Layout

Let's begin on a trip to examine the fundamental aspects that make up your Motorola Edge 50 Fusion's physical shape.

Front Panel: This is the side of the phone that confronts you during usage. It's dominated by the vivid exhibit, which fills a substantial chunk of the real estate. A thin bezel could surround the display, and a tiny cutout at the top or integrated inside the display itself houses the front-facing camera for selfies and video calls. Depending on the model, you could find an earpiece for phone conversations positioned at the upper border of the front panel.

Back Panel: The back panel gives a look into the phone's design style. It's often created from glass or plastic with a smooth or textured surface, available in a range of colors. The rear camera system, frequently accompanied by an LED flash, is normally positioned in a central spot or towards the top of the back panel. Some versions could contain a fingerprint sensor for security reasons, conveniently situated lower on the rear panel for easy access with your index finger.

Sides: The sides of the phone hold different buttons and ports that play vital roles in running your smartphone. The power button, responsible for turning the phone on and off, is normally situated on the right side. The volume rocker, a combination of two buttons that regulate the media volume and ringtone volume, could be positioned above or below the power button. On certain models, you could discover a dedicated button for accessing Google Assistant, the virtual assistant incorporated inside the Android operating system. The SIM card tray and microSD card slot (if applicable) are normally tucked away on the side of the phone, accessible using the included SIM card ejector tool.

Top and Bottom: The top and bottom borders of the phone could hold extra hardware components depending on the model. The microphone, used for collecting audio during calls and video recordings, is frequently positioned at the top or bottom edge. The USB-C connector, the principal port for charging the phone and transmitting data to and from a computer, is normally situated at the bottom edge. Some versions could contain a 3.5mm headphone socket on the bottom edge, enabling you to attach wired headphones.

Exploring the Display: Your Visual Gateway

The display of your Motorola Edge 50 Fusion acts as the window to your digital world. It lets you see images, watch movies, access applications, and interact with the phone's UI. Here's a deeper look at the display's functionalities:

 Display Technology: Your phone's display can employ OLED (Organic Light-Emitting Diode) or IPS LCD (In-Plane Switching

Liquid Crystal Display) technology. OLED displays provide deeper blacks and more brilliant colours, whereas IPS LCD screens are often more cheap and offer superior viewing angles.

Touchscreen Functionality: The display is a touchscreen, meaning you can interact with the phone's interface by tapping, swiping, pinching, and dragging your fingers over the surface. These motions enable you to browse menus, pick icons, and modify on-screen components.

Resolution and Clarity: The display resolution refers to the amount of pixels that make up the picture. A greater resolution corresponds to a crisper and more detailed image. The actual resolution of your phone's display will depend on the brand, but typical choices include HD+ (1600 x 720 pixels) and FHD+ (2300 x 1080 pixels).

Refresh Rate: The refresh rate refers to how frequently the display changes the picture on the screen per second. A faster refresh rate gives a smoother and more fluid visual experience, particularly visible while scrolling through material or playing games. Common refresh rates include 60Hz and 90Hz, with some models delivering even higher refresh rates for a very smooth experience.

Understanding the Buttons and Ports

The buttons and ports on your Motorola Edge 50 Fusion have diverse roles and are necessary for operating the smartphone. Here's a breakdown of their functions:

Power Button: As discussed previously, the power button is normally positioned on the right side of the phone. Pressing and holding it turns the phone on or off. A brief push on the power button could also wake the phone from sleep mode or lock the screen to prevent accidental touches.

Volume Rocker: The volume rocker is generally a set of two buttons positioned on the side of the phone, one for boosting the volume and another for reducing it. They regulate the media volume for music, films, games, and ringtones. You may also alter the ringer level for incoming calls and alerts.

Dedicated Google Assistant Button (Optional): Some Motorola Edge 50 Fusion versions can offer a dedicated button for activating Google Assistant. A single push or long press (depending on your settings) enables Google Assistant, enabling you to use voice commands to operate your phone, search for information, or accomplish tasks.

SIM Card Tray and microSD Card Slot (if applicable): The SIM card tray, normally found on the side of the phone, stores the SIM card issued by your mobile network provider. The SIM card allows you access to cellular network services including calls, text messaging, and mobile data. Some models could have a second microSD card slot, enabling you to extend the phone's storage space for extra photographs, movies, and information. You'll need to buy a microSD card separately (not included with the phone).

USB-C Port: The USB-C port, positioned near the bottom of the phone in most situations, serves numerous uses. It's the main charging connector, where you attach the accompanying charging cable and power adapter to charge your phone's battery. The USB-C connector also enables you to transmit data to and from a computer. You may connect the phone to a computer using a USB-C connector to transfer images, movies, music, and other media. Some USB-C connections also feature video output, enabling you to connect your phone to a TV or monitor to show the phone's screen on a bigger screen.

3.5mm Headphone Jack (Optional): Not all Motorola Edge 50 Fusion versions contain a 3.5mm headphone jack. If your model contains one, it's normally positioned near the bottom edge of the phone. The 3.5mm headphone connection lets wired headphones listen to music, view movies, or make calls.

Unlocking the Power of Security: Fingerprint Sensor and Options

Security is crucial when it comes to your smartphone. The Motorola Edge 50 Fusion provides numerous choices to preserve your smartphone and protect your data. Here's a closer look at the fingerprint sensor and other security features:

Fingerprint Sensor (Optional): Some Motorola Edge 50 Fusion models have a fingerprint sensor, often situated on the rear panel or embedded into the display. This sensor enables you to unlock your phone securely using your fingerprint. Enrolling your fingerprint includes putting your finger on the sensor many times throughout the setup procedure. Once registered, you can just rest your finger on the sensor to unlock the phone fast and effortlessly.

Pin, Pattern, or Password: In addition to the fingerprint sensor (if available), you may set up a PIN (Personal Identification Number), pattern, or password as a screen lock mechanism. A PIN is a numerical code you input to unlock the screen. A pattern includes drawing a precise series of dots on the screen to unlock. A password is a combination of letters, numbers, and symbols used for unlocking. Setting a strong PIN, pattern, or password is vital for added protection in case the fingerprint sensor breaks or you prefer an alternative unlock method.

facial Recognition (Optional): Some models could feature facial recognition as an additional unlock option. This technology leverages the front-facing camera to detect your face and unlock the phone appropriately. While handy, face recognition may not be as safe as fingerprint sensors or PINs.

Secure Lock Settings: Within the phone's security settings, you may modify many parts of your screen lock and security features. You may modify the lock screen timeout, which controls how long the phone remains unlocked after inactivity before prompting you to input your PIN, pattern, or password again. You may also activate features like "Find My Device" from Google, which helps find your lost or stolen phone, and "Factory Reset Protection," which involves inputting your Google account credentials before resetting the phone to factory settings.

By knowing the structure of your Motorola Edge o Fusion's hardware, the functions of the display, and the various security choices, you're well-equipped to manage your phone with confidence and keep your data secure. The next chapters will go further into the software features and functions, allowing you to unleash the full potential of your smartphone.

CHAPTER 4

Unveiling the Software of Your Motorola Edge 50 Fusion

The Motorola Edge 50 Fusion relies on the Android operating system, a user-friendly platform powering millions of smartphones worldwide. This chapter sheds light on the essential capabilities of Android, helping you through browsing the home screen, handling alerts, and customising your phone's look.

Understanding the Android Ecosystem

Android, created by Google, acts as the backbone for your Motorola Edge 50 Fusion's software. It delivers the essential features you depend on, from making calls and sending messages to running programmes and accessing the internet.

Here's a summary of essential components of the Android operating system:

Open Source Foundation: Android is built on an open-source platform, enabling manufacturers like Motorola to alter it while adhering to a basic set of features. This results to a familiar experience across various Android devices with minor changes based on the manufacturer's modifications.

Intuitive design: Android features a user-friendly design that stresses simplicity of use. The home screen acts as your core hub, while natural gestures let you browse between applications and menus with ease.

App-Centric Experience: The main strength of Android comes in its large app ecosystem. The Google Play Store provides millions of applications, divided into numerous categories including gaming, social networking, productivity tools, and more. These applications increase your phone's capabilities and adapt to your specific demands.

Regular Updates: Google constantly distributes updates to the Android operating system, providing new features, security patches, and bug fixes. Your Motorola Edge 50 Fusion will get these updates over time, ensuring your smartphone remains safe and up-to-date.

Navigating the Home Screen: Your Launchpad to Action

The home screen is the beginning point for interacting with your phone. It shows app icons, widgets (miniature applications that allow rapid access to information or functionalities), and a search bar. Here's how to browse this core hub:

App Icons: These coloured squares or icons indicate the applications loaded on your phone. Tapping an icon starts the related app. You may rearrange app icons by long-pressing on an icon and dragging it to a new spot on the home screen.

Widgets: These give easy methods to see information or execute tasks without launching a complete app. Examples are weather widgets that indicate the current temperature, calendar widgets that show future events, and music player widgets that enable you to control music playing. Long-press on an empty area of the home screen to enter the widget selection menu and pick the widgets you wish to add.

Dock: The dock is normally situated at the bottom of the home screen and may house a few commonly used app icons for easy access. You may edit the applications shown in the dock by long-pressing on an icon in the dock and replacing it with another app.

Search Bar: The search bar, commonly positioned at the top of the home screen, enables you to easily discover installed applications or search the web using Google. Simply put your search query into the bar and hit the magnifying glass symbol or the "Search" button on the keyboard to commence your search.

Swiping for Efficiency: Mastering Gestures

Mastering gestures is crucial to managing your phone effectively. Here are some crucial swipes to remember:

Swiping Up: Swiping upwards from the bottom of the home screen opens the app drawer, which shows a list of all your installed applications.

Swiping Left or Right: By default, swiping left or right across the home screen navigates between various home screen pages. You may modify the amount of home screen pages later on.

Swiping Down: Swiping down from the top of the screen exposes the notification panel. This panel shows alerts and notifications from applications, as well as fast settings for regularly used functionalities like Wi-Fi, Bluetooth, and brightness.

Understanding the Notification Panel: Staying Informed

The notification panel keeps you informed about crucial notifications and app updates. Here's how to access and manage it:

Swiping Down: Swipe down from the top of the screen to see the notification panel. This panel shows notifications in a chronological manner, with the most recent notifications showing at the top.

Clearing Notifications: Tap the "X" button in the corner of each notification to clear it separately. You may also slide the notice to the left or right to dismiss it.

fast Settings: The top area of the notification panel commonly holds fast settings icons for Wi-Fi, Bluetooth, flashlight, and other frequently used services. Tap an icon to turn its status on or off. You may expand this area by swiping down twice to display more fast settings choices.

Customizing Your Phone: Express Yourself

The beauty of Android resides in the flexibility to tailor your experience. Here are ways to alter the appearance and feel of your Motorola Edge 50 Fusion:

Changing the Wallpaper: The wallpaper is the background picture you view on your home screen. You may modify it to fit your style. Long-press on an empty space of the home screen and pick "Wallpaper" from the menu. You may pick from pre-loaded backgrounds or choose a new picture from your collection.

Setting Custom Ringtones and Notifications: Tired of the default ringtones and notification sounds? You may change them to suit your tastes. Navigate to your phone's settings menu and find the "Sounds & vibration" section. Here, you may pick new ringtones for calls and text messages, as well as notification sounds for various applications.

Themes (Optional): Some Motorola Edge 50 Fusion models could provide downloaded themes that modify the overall appearance and feel of the user interface. Themes may adjust the background, app icons, fonts, and even system noises, creating a coherent design. Explore the theme choices under your phone's settings or the Google Play Store to find themes that resonate with you.

Customizing the App Drawer: You may arrange your app drawer for quicker navigation. Most Android phones enable you to organise applications alphabetically, by most recently used, or by custom categories. Within the settings menu, find the "Home screen" or "Apps" section and explore the different sorting choices for the app drawer.

Adding Widgets Strategically: Widgets provide a quick method to access information and functions at a glance.

While adding widgets may customise your home screen, it's vital to establish a balance to minimise clutter. Experiment with various widget positions and pick the ones that give the greatest value for your everyday usage.

Unlocking the Power of Apps

Now that you've mastered the essential features of the Android UI, let's plunge into the realm of applications. Apps are the heart and soul of the Android experience, delivering a huge number of features to improve your phone's capabilities.

The Google Play Store: The Google Play Store acts as your one-stop shop for finding and downloading applications. It has millions of applications, classified into numerous sectors including gaming, social networking, productivity tools, entertainment, and more. You may explore the Play Store by category, search for individual applications by name, or read reviews before downloading.

Installing and Managing Apps: Once you've discovered an app that interests you on the Play Store, just hit the "Install" button. The app will download and install into your phone. You can manage your installed applications under the settings menu. Here, you may check app details, update programmes to their newest versions, or delete apps you no longer need.

Keeping Apps Updated: App updates typically provide new features, bug fixes, and security enhancements. It's vital to keep your applications updated for best performance and security. The Play Store may tell you when updates are available for your loaded applications. You may also manually check for updates inside the Play Store app.

By learning the Android operating system, navigating the home screen and app drawer, controlling alerts, and customizing the appearance and feel of your phone, you've made a huge step towards mastering your Motorola Edge 50 Fusion. The next chapters will examine particular capabilities like making calls, sending messages, managing contacts, and using the power of the camera, equipping you to unleash the full potential of your smartphone.

CHAPTER 5

Connecting with the World: Making Calls and Texting

Your Motorola Edge 50 Fusion is more than simply a smartphone; it's a communication powerhouse. This chapter offers you the skills to make calls, send text messages, and keep connected with your loved ones and coworkers.

Placing and Receiving Calls: The Essence of Communication

The Phone App: The Phone app acts as your core hub for making and receiving calls.

Locate the Phone app icon on your home screen or app drawer and press to launch it.

The Dial Pad: The dial pad, displayed prominently inside the Phone app, allowing you to input phone numbers manually. Tap the numbers on the dial pad to form the phone number you want to call.

Initiating a Call: Once you've typed the phone number on the dial pad, hit the green phone symbol (typically situated at the bottom center of the screen) to begin the call. Your phone will begin calling the number, and if the call connects, you may talk with the receiver.

The Call Screen: During a call, the call screen shows information about the call, such as the caller ID (if available) and the call length. You'll also discover buttons to mute the microphone, engage speakerphone, open the call options menu (providing features like holding the call or adding another person for a conference call), and terminate the conversation.

Receiving Calls: When someone calls you, your phone will ring and show information about the caller on the screen. You'll notice choices to accept the call by swiping upwards on the green answer button or refuse the call by swiping upwards on the red decline button. You may also mute the ringtone by tapping the volume down button.

Recent Calls: The Phone app retains a call history, detailing your recent incoming and outgoing calls. Tap on a call entry to examine data including the date, time, and call length. You may also start a call back to the same number from the call history.

The Contacts App: Your Address Book

The Contacts app keeps information about the individuals you connect with often. It serves as your digital address book, enabling you to conveniently search and call people.

Adding Contacts: There are various methods to add contacts to your phone. You may manually input their name, phone number, email address, and other data inside the Contacts app. You may also import contacts from your old phone or social media accounts.

Editing Contacts: Your contact information could change over time. The Contacts app enables you to change existing entries, update phone numbers, add email addresses, or adjust other data.

Searching for Contacts: With a big number of contacts, identifying a particular individual might be time-consuming. The Contacts app contains a search box that enables you to search for contacts by name or phone number. Simply start entering the name or number, and relevant contacts will show on the screen.

Favorites: For regularly called contacts, you may add them to your Favorites list inside the Contacts app. This generates a fast access list, enabling you to summon them with a single press.

The Art of Texting: Sending and Receiving Messages

Texting, also known as SMS (brief Message Service) or MMS (Multimedia Messaging Service), enables you to send brief messages to other phones. Here's how to master the art of messaging on your Motorola Edge 50 Fusion:

The Messaging App: The Messaging app acts as your centre for sending and receiving text messages. Locate the Messaging app icon on your home screen or app drawer and press to activate it.

Composing a New Text: To begin a new text message, hit the compose button (typically a plus sign symbol) inside the Messaging app. This opens a new message window where you may input the recipient's phone number or pick a person from your address book.

Crafting Your Message: Once you've added the recipient, you can construct your message in the text box at the bottom of the screen. The keyboard enables you to input your message. You may also use emojis (expressive symbols) to improve your message.

Sending a Text: When your message is ready, touch the send button (typically an arrow icon) to send the text message to the receiver. Depending on your network provider, you could obtain a notice indicating that the message has been delivered.

Receiving Text Messages: When you get a text message, a notice will show on your phone, displaying the sender's name or number and a fragment of the message. Tap on the notice to access the message and read it in its full.

Conversation Threads: Text message discussions are divided into threads. Each thread holds the whole communication history between you and the receiver. This enables you to simply follow the course of the discussion and examine prior messages exchanged.

MMS (Multimedia Messaging Service): In addition to text messages, you can also send multimedia messages (MMS) using the Messaging app. MMS enables you to transmit images, videos, music files, and even virtual stickers to other compatible phones. To send an MMS, just hit the paperclip icon or the "+" sign inside the compose window and attach the chosen media file. Be warned that MMS messages could incur extra costs from your network provider depending on your package.

Exploring Additional Messaging Features:

The realm of texting goes beyond mere text messages. Here are some other features you may find useful:

Group Messaging: Texting isn't confined to one-on-one chats. You may build group messages to deliver a message to numerous recipients concurrently. This is perfect for keeping a group of friends or coworkers informed on a common event or plan.

Emojis and Stickers: Emojis and stickers offer a touch of personality and individuality to your text messages. Your Motorola Edge 50 Fusion likely comes pre-loaded with a number of emojis. You may also download more emoji packs or sticker applications from the Google Play Store to enhance your selections.

Customizing Notifications: You may adjust notification sounds and ringtones for specific contacts or messaging groups. This enables you to readily identify who's messaging you without having to glance at your phone.

Blocking Numbers: If you're getting unwelcome texts from a certain number, you may block that number from the Messaging app. This will prohibit you from getting future texts from that number.

By learning the functions of the Phone and Messaging applications, you've provided yourself with the vital tools for remaining connected with the world around you. The next chapters will go further into various features of your Motorola Edge 50 Fusion, allowing you to explore the camera, manage your multimedia files, and browse the internet with confidence.

CHAPTER 6

Capturing Memories: The Power of the Motorola Edge 50 Fusion Camera

Your Motorola Edge 50 Fusion offers a flexible camera system, letting you create amazing images and movies of life's moments. This chapter offers you the knowledge to unlock the camera's potential and produce share-worthy material.

Unveiling the Camera App:

The camera app acts as your doorway to taking images and movies. Locate the Camera app icon on your home screen or app drawer and press to launch it. The camera app interface commonly shows the following elements:

Viewfinder: The viewfinder fills the bulk of the screen and offers a live glimpse of what the camera lens sees. This is where you frame your shot and compose your images or films.

Capture Button: The capture button, commonly a big circular button positioned in the bottom centre of the screen, is your trigger for taking images and movies. A simple touch snaps a picture, while a lengthy hold on the capture button enables video recording.

Switch Camera Button: This button, commonly symbolised by an arrow or camera icon, enables you to switch between the rear-facing camera (used for recording images and movies of the world around you) and the front-facing camera (used for shooting selfies).

Mode Switcher: The mode switcher, generally represented by a carousel symbol or swiping left and right on the screen, gives access to several camera modes. These modes provide unique features for recording different sorts of images and movies.

Settings Button: The settings button, often displayed by a gear icon, allows access to the camera app's settings menu. Here, you may alter numerous camera specifications including resolution, flash settings, and focus choices.

Exploring Camera Modes:

The camera app provides several settings to adapt to diverse shooting circumstances. Here's a summary of several typical camera modes:

Photo: This is the default setting, great for capturing ordinary moments. Simply compose your shot and hit the capture button to snap a picture.

Portrait: This setting blurs the backdrop behind your subject, providing a professional-looking portrait impression. This option is perfect for shooting images of people or objects when you want to highlight the subject against a blurred backdrop.

Night Vision: Struggling to shoot clear images in low-light conditions? Night Vision mode incorporates software processing to boost brightness and clarity in low light areas. However, take in aware that night vision photographs could display some graininess.

Video: This mode enables you to record videos. hit the capture button once to start recording and hit it again to stop. While filming, you may zoom in and out by pinching or spreading your fingers on the screen.

Pro Mode (Optional): For photography lovers, certain Motorola Edge 50 Fusion versions can have a Pro mode. This mode allows granular control over camera parameters like shutter speed, ISO, and white balance, enabling you to fine-tune your images for unique artistic effects.

Mastering the Art of the Selfie

The front-facing camera of the Motorola Edge 50 Fusion lets you to shoot selfies and engage in video conversations. Here's how to use it effectively:

Switching to the Front Camera: Locate the switch camera button and press it to switch to the front-facing camera. The viewfinder will now show your own picture.

Framing Your Selfie: Hold your phone at arm's length or use the selfie stick (available separately) for a larger field of vision. You may also utilise the volume rocker buttons on the side of your phone to snap the selfie instead of utilising the on-screen capture button.

Portrait option (Optional): Some models could include a portrait option for the front-facing camera as well. This option blurs the backdrop behind you, producing a more professional selfie image.

Mirror Image versus. Original: By default, the taken selfie could seem mirrored. You may alter this behavior inside the camera settings to store selfies in their original position.

Editing and Sharing Your Creations

Once you've recorded photographs and videos, you may wish to edit or share them.

Here's how to improve your projects and share them with the world:

The Gallery App: The Gallery app acts as your picture and video collection. All your collected photographs and videos are kept here, enabling you to view, modify, and share them.

Editing options: The Gallery app frequently includes with basic editing options including cropping, rotating, and altering brightness and contrast. You may also use filters to add creative touches to your images. Some models could provide more powerful editing options inside the Gallery app.

Sharing Options: Once you've modified your photographs or movies to your taste, you may share them with friends, family, or the broader world via several platforms. Here are some popular sharing options:

Social Media: Share your photographs and videos straight on social media networks like Facebook, Instagram, Twitter, or TikTok. Simply pick the chosen platform from the sharing option inside the Gallery app and follow the on-screen directions to log in and submit your masterpiece.

Messaging applications: Send your photographs and videos to friends or family using messaging applications like WhatsApp, Telegram, or Messenger. Select the messaging app from the sharing menu and pick the recipient(s) to share your photographs or videos.

Email: Attach your photographs and videos to emails and distribute them to your contacts. Open the email app, create a new message, press the paperclip button to attach files, then pick the photographs or videos you wish to send.

Cloud Storage Services: Upload your photographs and movies to cloud storage services like Google photographs or Dropbox. This enables you to back up your projects online and access them from any device with an internet connection.

Additional Camera Tips and Tricks

Here are some extra suggestions to help you shoot amazing photographs and movies with your Motorola Edge 50 Fusion:

Pay Attention to Lighting: Good lighting is vital for getting clear and colourful photographs. Whenever feasible, try to snap images in natural lighting for maximum effects.

Focus on Your topic: Tap on the screen to adjust the focus on your primary topic, particularly when using Portrait mode or when your subject is off-center.

Steady Your Hand: Camera shaking might lead to grainy photographs. Hold your phone firmly or use a tripod for more stable images, particularly in low-light circumstances.

Explore new Angles: Don't be scared to experiment with new shooting angles. Sometimes, a distinctive angle may add visual appeal to your images.

Burst Mode (Optional): Some models could provide a burst mode that snaps many photographs in fast succession. This is great for capturing fast-moving subjects or action photographs.

study Your images: Take a minute to study your images after taking them. This helps you to spot any possible faults and retake the shot if required.

By knowing the camera app's features, exploring various camera settings, and employing editing and sharing options, you're well on your way to being a mobile photography expert with your Motorola Edge 50 Fusion. The subsequent chapters will dig into further multimedia functions, help you through managing your files, and equip you to explore the web with ease.

CHAPTER 7

Unveiling the World Wide Web

The internet delivers a wide world of knowledge, entertainment, and conversation at your fingertips. This chapter prepares you with the expertise to connect your Motorola Edge 50 Fusion to the web and access the unlimited possibilities of the internet.

Connecting to Wi-Fi Networks: Your Gateway to the Web

Wi-Fi networks enable wireless internet connectivity, frequently found in homes, workplaces, and public hotspots. Here's how to connect your phone to a Wi-Fi network:

Accessing Wi-Fi Settings: Swipe down from the top of the screen to open the notification panel. Locate the Wi-Fi icon and press it to switch on Wi-Fi. Alternatively, browse to your phone's settings menu and select the "Wi-Fi" option.

Searching for Networks: With Wi-Fi enabled, your phone will check for accessible Wi-Fi networks in your neighbourhood. A list of recognised networks will show on the screen, indicating the network name (SSID) and signal strength.

Joining a Network: Tap on the chosen Wi-Fi network from the list. If the network is password-protected, you'll be requested to enter the password. Once input properly, your phone will connect to the Wi-Fi network, and you'll be able to access the internet.

Saved Networks: Your phone remembers previously connected Wi-Fi networks along with their credentials. This enables you to automatically connect to known networks without re-entering the password each time.

Mobile Data: Accessing the Web On-the-Go (if applicable)

While Wi-Fi networks provide a stable internet connection, they may not always be accessible. Depending on your cell network provider plan, you could have access to mobile data. Mobile data exploits your cellular network's data connection to access the internet.

Enabling Mobile Data: Navigate to your phone's settings menu and select the "Mobile network" or "Data usage" option. Here, you'll find an option to activate or disable mobile data. Activating mobile data enables your phone to connect to the internet via your cellular network.

Data consumption Monitoring: Mobile data consumption might incur costs based on your plan. It's vital to check your data consumption to prevent surpassing your plan's restrictions. Your phone settings normally show information about your mobile data consumption, enabling you to monitor how much data you've spent. You may also set data use limitations to get warnings when you're nearing your plan's limit.

Connecting via Bluetooth: Pairing with Other Devices

Bluetooth is a short-range wireless technology that enables your Motorola Edge 50 Fusion to communicate with other Bluetooth-enabled devices. Here are some popular Bluetooth use cases:

Wireless Headphones and Speakers: Pair your phone with wireless headphones or speakers to enjoy music, podcasts, and audiobooks without the inconvenience of cords.

Sharing things: Transfer things like photographs, movies, and documents between your phone and other Bluetooth-enabled devices like PCs or other phones.

Car Hands-Free: Connect your phone to your car's Bluetooth system for hands-free calling and music streaming while driving.

Wearable Devices: Pair your phone with smartwatches or fitness trackers to get alerts, monitor your health statistics, and control music playing.

Pairing a Device: Navigate to the Bluetooth settings on your phone. Enable Bluetooth and verify the target device is discoverable (generally accessible to other devices for connection). Your phone will scan for accessible Bluetooth devices. Select the device you wish to link with and follow any on-screen instructions to finish the pairing procedure.

Exploring the Web with Chrome: Your Window to the World

The Google Chrome web browser is pre-installed on your Motorola Edge 50 Fusion, acting as your entrance to explore the great expanse of the internet. Here's how to browse Chrome:

Launching Chrome: Locate the Chrome icon on your home screen or app drawer and press to activate the browser.

The Address Bar: The address bar at the top of the screen shows the web address (URL) of the currently loaded website. You may put a URL straight into the address bar to browse to a certain website.

Search Bar: The address bar typically acts as a search bar. Type your search phrase into the bar and touch the search icon (magnifying glass) or click the "Enter" key on the keyboard to conduct an online search using Google.

Navigation Buttons: Chrome shows forward and back buttons to move through your browser history. You may return previously accessible sites or go back a step in your browsing trip.

Tabs: Chrome enables you to open many websites concurrently in different tabs. This allows you to effortlessly move between multiple websites without having to shut them fully. Tap the "Tabs" icon (typically a square with stacked rectangles) to see and manage your open tabs.

Bookmarks: Bookmarking enables you to keep favorite websites for convenient access in the future. Navigate to the relevant website, press the three-dot menu symbol in the upper right corner, and choose "Add bookmark" to store the webpage for later reference. You may access your bookmarks by touching the three-dot menu symbol again and choosing "Bookmarks."

surfing Modes: Chrome provides multiple surfing modes to increase your privacy and security. Regular browsing mode is suited for most ordinary work. Incognito mode enables you to surf the web discreetly, avoiding browser history from being kept on your device.

Staying Secure While Browsing

The internet may be a wonderful source of knowledge, but it's also vital to practice care when surfing. Here are some strategies for remaining secure:

Beware of Phishing Sites: Phishing websites seek to fool you into providing personal information or clicking on dangerous links. Be aware of websites that seem dubious or seek crucial information unexpectedly.

Download Apps Only from Trusted Sources: Only download apps from the official Google Play Store to limit the chance of malware infestations. Avoid downloading programmes from unknown websites or third-party app shops.

Keep Your Software Updated: Regular software updates typically contain security patches that resolve vulnerabilities. Ensure your phone's operating system and applications are updated to the newest versions to ensure maximum security.

Use Strong Passwords: Create strong and unique passwords for your online accounts. Avoid using easily guessable passwords or the same password for multiple accounts. Consider using a password manager to generate and store strong passwords securely.

By understanding how to connect to Wi-Fi networks, utilize mobile data (if applicable), pair with Bluetooth devices, and navigate the Chrome web browser, you've unlocked the door to exploring the vast potential of the internet on your Motorola Edge 50 Fusion. The following chapters will delve into managing your files, exploring multimedia functionalities like music and videos, and navigating the exciting world of apps.

CHAPTER 8

Unleashing Entertainment: Music, Videos, Games, and More

Your Motorola Edge 50 Fusion isn't just a communication tool; it's a portable entertainment powerhouse. This chapter prepares you to use its multimedia features, play music and films, explore games, and uncover a world of entertainment alternatives.

Playing Music and Videos: Taking Your Tunes and Shows On-the-Go

The Stock Music Player: Your Motorola Edge 50 Fusion likely comes pre-installed with a music player app. This software enables you to play music files saved on your phone's internal storage or microSD card (if appropriate). Locate the music player app icon and press to activate it.

Adding Music to Your Library: The music player software checks your phone's storage for music files and shows them in its library. You may also manually add music files by moving them from your computer or obtaining them from reputable sources.

Playback Controls: The music player software has playback controls that enable you to play, stop, skip songs, change the volume, and shuffle or repeat your playlist. Explore the app's UI to acquaint yourself with these controls.

making Playlists: Organize your music collection by making playlists. Playlists enable you to organise your favorite music together for convenient access. Most music player applications enable you to create, update, and remove playlists.

The Gallery App for Videos: The Gallery app, which keeps your images, sometimes serves as a video player. Locate your video files inside the Gallery app and touch on them to commence playing. The Gallery app includes basic playback options for movies, letting you to play, stop, modify volume, and alter video playback speed (on certain models).

Third-Party Music and movie Players: The Google Play Store provides a range of music and movie player applications with extra capabilities. Explore the Play Store to find music players with features like equalisation settings, lyrics display, or interaction with streaming providers. Similarly, video player applications could feature complex playback settings, subtitle support, or video casting capabilities.

Exploring Multimedia Apps and Games: A World of Entertainment Awaits

The Google Play Store serves as your doorway to a large library of entertainment alternatives. Here's how to plunge into this amazing world:

Accessing the Play Store: Locate the Play Store app icon on your home screen or app drawer and press to start it. The Play Store categorizes applications and games into numerous areas, making it simple to locate what you're searching for.

Downloading and Installing Apps and Games: When you discover an app or game that interests you, touch on it to explore its information, including screenshots, ratings, and reviews. If you opt to download it, touch the "Install" button. The software or game will download and install into your phone. Once the installation is complete, you'll find the app or game icon on your home screen or app drawer, ready to begin.

In-App Purchases (IAP): Be cautious that certain applications and games can offer in-app purchases (IAP) for extra features, virtual objects, or upgrades. These transactions are normally made using your Google Play Store payment method. Always study the IAP information before making any purchases, particularly if you're giving your phone to a youngster.

Parental Controls: The Play Store features parental controls that enable you to block access to adult material or applications requiring in-app payments. Explore your phone's settings menu to locate and configure parental controls for the Play Store.

Unleashing the Power of Streaming Services

Streaming services offer on-demand access to a vast library of music, movies, TV shows, and even live television. Here's how to leverage streaming services on your Motorola Edge 50 Fusion:

Subscribing to Streaming Services: Numerous streaming services cater to different interests and budgets. Popular options include Spotify, YouTube Music, Netflix, Hulu, Disney+, and HBO Max. Each service typically requires a monthly subscription fee. Explore the offerings of different streaming services to find one that aligns with your preferences.

Downloading Streaming Apps: Once you've subscribed to a streaming service, download its app from the Google Play Store. Launch the app, log in with your account credentials, and start exploring the available content library.

Downloading for Offline Viewing (Optional): Some streaming services allow you to download movies or TV shows for offline viewing. This is particularly useful when travelling or in areas with limited internet connectivity. Locate the download option within the specific streaming service app to download content for offline enjoyment.

Taking Advantage of Built-in Entertainment Features

Your Motorola Edge 50 Fusion can come with pre-loaded entertainment functions beyond music and video playback. Here are some instances to explore:

FM Radio: Enjoy live radio broadcasts on the move with the built-in FM radio app (if available on your model). Tune into your favorite channels and find new music, news, or discussion programmes.

Games Hub (Optional): Some Motorola Edge 50 Fusion devices can contain a Games Hub app. This app curates a range of pre-installed casual games or gives suggestions for downloading games from the Play Store.

Screen Mirroring: Cast your phone's screen to a suitable TV or monitor utilising screen mirroring technology (Miracast or Chromecast). This lets you watch movies, videos, or even games on a bigger screen for an improved entertainment experience. Explore your phone's settings menu to identify and set up screen mirroring features.

Optimizing Your Entertainment Experience

Here are some ways to optimise your pleasure when using your Motorola Edge 50 Fusion for entertainment:

Investing in Headphones or Speakers: A decent set of headphones or portable speakers may dramatically improve your music and audio experience. Explore numerous alternatives depending on your budget and interests.

Managing Storage Space: Downloading music, films, and games may use storage space on your phone. Monitor your storage utilisation and consider eliminating obsolete files or transferring them to a microSD card (if applicable) to free up space for new stuff.

Adjusting Display Settings: For ideal video watching, modify your phone's display settings like brightness and contrast to fit your tastes and viewing situation. Some devices could provide display settings particularly tailored for video playback.

Taking rests: While the Motorola Edge 50 Fusion provides a wealth of entertainment alternatives, remember to take rests to minimise eye strain or ignoring other obligations.

By comprehending the built-in music and video players, exploring the enormous universe of applications and games on the Play Store, utilising streaming services, and taking use of pre-loaded entertainment features, you've made your Motorola Edge 50 Fusion into a flexible entertainment centre. The next chapter will go into managing your files and data, ensuring your phone stays organized and efficient.

Chapter 9: Conquering Your Day: Staying Organized and Productive

Your Motorola Edge 50 Fusion is more than just a communication and entertainment device; it's a strong tool for keeping organized and improving your work. This chapter gives you the knowledge to leverage built-in applications and discover other alternatives to manage your calendar, make reminders, and tackle your to-do list.

Mastering Your Time: The Calendar App

The Calendar app acts as your primary centre for scheduling appointments, activities, and deadlines. Here's how to browse and use it effectively:

Launching the Calendar App: Locate the Calendar app icon on your home screen or app drawer and press to activate it. The calendar app normally shows the current month in a grid style, with each date block representing a day.

Viewing multiple Calendar Views: The Calendar software typically enables you to move between multiple calendar views. You may examine the full month at a glance, switch to a weekly view for a more extensive breakdown, or even select for a daily agenda view to see your scheduled activities for the exact day.

Adding New Events: Tap on the chosen date inside the calendar pane to create a new event. This will open a new event creation box where you can input data like the event title, date, time, length, location (optional), and even invite participants (if the event includes others).

Setting Reminders: Ensure you don't miss crucial occasions by setting reminders. While creating a new event, look for the option to "Add reminder" or "Set notification." Choose how far in advance you want to be alerted before the event, and your phone will notify you at the chosen time.

regular activities: Do you have regular activities like meetings or seminars on a fixed schedule? The calendar software enables you to establish recurring events, saving you time from manually inputting the same data over. Set the frequency of the repeating event (daily, weekly, monthly, etc.) when establishing the event.

Syncing Calendars (Optional): If you use other calendar services like Google Calendar or Outlook, you may connect your Motorola Edge 50 Fusion's calendar app with those services. This guarantees all your activities are shown in one single area, reducing the need to maintain several calendars. Explore your phone's settings menu to discover calendar synchronisation options.

Remembering the Important Stuff: Reminders and To-Do Lists

Your Motorola Edge 50 Fusion is loaded with features to help you recall things and keep on top of your to-do list. Here's how to employ them:

The Built-in Reminders App: Some Motorola Edge 50 Fusion models can contain a dedicated Reminders app. This programme enables you to make easy reminders for jobs, errands, or anything you don't want to forget. Set a reminder with a title, date, and time, and your phone will inform you when the reminder becomes due.

Creating Notes with Reminders: The built-in Notes app (available on all models) may be more than simply a note-taking tool. While composing a note, search for an option to "Add reminder." This changes your note into a reminder with a specified date and time notice.

Third-Party To-Do List applications: The Google Play Store provides a broad range of to-do list applications with extensive functionality. Explore these applications to uncover functionality like work prioritising, recurring to-dos, collaborative features, and interaction with other productivity tools.

Taking Notes on the Go: The Notes App

The Notes app enables you to record thoughts, write down vital information, or make shopping lists. Here's how to get started:

Launching the Notes App: Locate the Notes app icon on your home screen or app drawer and press to activate it. The software generally shows a list of previous notes or gives a blank note for you to begin composing.

Creating a New Note: Tap the "New note" button (typically a plus sign symbol) to make a new note. Start inputting your note content, which may comprise text, bulleted lists, numbered lists, or even graphics (on certain models).

Organizing Your Notes: With several notes, keeping them organized becomes vital. Some Notes programmes enable you to create folders or notebooks to classify your notes by subject. You may also rename notes or add labels for easy identification.

Sharing Notes (Optional): The Notes app could give choices to share your notes with others. This might be beneficial for collaborating on projects or exchanging shopping lists with family members. Explore sharing options within the exact Notes app you're using.

Expanding Your Productivity Toolkit: Exploring Additional Apps

The Google Play Store provides a myriad of productivity applications to appeal to diverse demands. Here are some instances to explore:

Project Management tools: If you handle complicated projects, try project management tools like Asana, Trello, or Monday.com. These applications include features like task delegation, progress monitoring, file sharing, and communication tools to optimise project operations.

Time Management Apps: Apps like RescueTime or Focus Keeper may help you manage your time successfully. These applications analyse your phone use habits or apply the Pomodoro Technique (work periods with brief breaks) to increase your attention and productivity.

File Management Apps: While your phone comes with a built-in file manager, investigate choices like ES File Explorer or Solid Explorer for sophisticated file management functionality. These tools enable you to classify files, compress or extract archives, and use cloud storage services for efficient file organising.

Note-Taking Apps with sophisticated functionality: For power users, note-taking apps like Evernote, OneNote, or Google Keep provide sophisticated functionality beyond the basic Notes app. These programmes allow for rich text formatting, picture or audio note attachments, handwriting recognition (on certain models), and syncing features across several devices.

Optimizing Your Workflow

Here are some suggestions to enhance your productivity with your Motorola Edge 50 Fusion:

Schedule Regularly: Block up designated time slots in your calendar software for concentrated work sessions or crucial activities. Treat these planned meetings like any other meeting to ensure you prioritize your to-do list.

Minimize Distractions: While your phone provides different entertainment alternatives, try silencing alerts or using Do Not Disturb mode while concentrating on vital activities. This eliminates distractions and helps you remain concentrated.

Sync Across Devices: Many productivity applications feature multi-device syncing capabilities. Sync your tasks, notes, and calendars across your phone, PC, and tablet to guarantee you have access to your information from any device.

examine and Revise: Regularly examine your to-do list, notes, and calendar to ensure you're on track with your objectives and priorities. Don't hesitate to change your schedule, assign work, or re-prioritize as required.

By mastering the built-in calendar software, employing reminders and to-do list choices, taking notes efficiently, and exploring other productivity applications, you've converted your Motorola Edge 50 Fusion into a strong tool for managing your time, conquering your responsibilities, and reaching your objectives. The next chapter will go into discovering the fascinating world of applications and accessing the massive content library of the Google Play Store.

CHAPTER 9

Safeguarding Your Sanctuary

There is a variety of personal information that is stored on your Motorola Edge 50 Fusion, including contacts, images, messages, and financial applications from your phone. Through reading this chapter, you will get the knowledge necessary to adopt key security measures, therefore protecting both your phone and your data.

Putting in place a screen lock and a password protection system is the first line of defence.

It is essential to have a screen lock in order to prevent unauthorised access to your phone and the information it contains. This is how you can put up a lock on your screen:

Accessing the Security Settings: To access the Security settings, go to the settings menu on your phone and select the "Security" or "Lock screen" section. There are a variety of choices available for customising your screen lock in this area.

Selecting a Method for Locking the Screen: You have access to a number of different screen lock techniques on your Motorola Edge 50 Fusion, each of which provides a different degree of protection. Here's a summary of typical options:

Swipe: This is the least secure option, requiring a simple swipe motion to unlock the screen. Although handy, it provides just a limited level of security.

PIN: A PIN (Personal Identification Number) involves inputting a series of digits to unlock the screen. Choose a strong PIN that's simple for you to remember but tough for others to guess. Avoid utilising basic patterns or birthdates.

Password: Similar to a PIN, a password combines a mix of letters, numbers, and symbols for greater security. Create a secure password that's at least 8 characters long and contains a combination of capital and lowercase letters, numbers, and symbols.

Pattern: Unlock your phone by sketching a specified pattern on the screen. While handy, patterns may be prone to smudges, making them potentially less secure than PINs or passwords.

Fingerprint Unlock (Optional): If your Motorola Edge 50 Fusion contains a fingerprint sensor, you may employ fingerprint recognition to unlock your phone securely. This approach employs your unique fingerprint for safe and easy screen unlocking.

Facial Recognition (Optional): Some models could provide facial recognition as a screen lock option. This approach employs the front-facing camera to scan your face and unlock the phone if it knows you. While handy, face recognition can be less secure than fingerprint unlocking in certain lighting circumstances.

Setting Up Your preferred technique: Follow the on-screen prompts to establish your preferred screen lock technique. This often entails generating a PIN, password, pattern, or registering your fingerprint or face for identification.

Auto-Lock: Activate the auto-lock option to guarantee your phone's screen automatically locks after a period of inactivity. This decreases the possibility of unwanted access if you leave your phone alone. You may alter the auto-lock timeout under the security settings menu.

Enhancing Security with Fingerprint or Facial Recognition (if available)

Fingerprint unlocking and face recognition provide simple and safe screen lock alternatives (on supported devices). Here's a closer look:

Fingerprint Unlocking: If your phone includes a fingerprint sensor, consider registering one or more fingerprints for unlocking. This solution employs your unique fingerprint for safe and rapid access. Ensure your fingers are clean and dry while registering your fingerprints for maximum sensor function.

Facial Recognition: Some models provide facial recognition as a screen lock option. While handy, it's crucial to recognise its limits. Facial recognition may not perform well in low-light circumstances or if you wear glasses, hats, or other facial coverings. For greater protection, try utilising face recognition in combination with a PIN or password as a backup approach.

Understanding App Permissions: Granting Access Wisely

When you install applications from the Google Play Store, they could seek permission to access specific features or data on your phone. Here's how to understand and manage app permissions:

Reviewing App Permissions: During app installation, pay attention to the permissions the programme is seeking. These rights could include access to your location, camera, microphone, contacts, storage, or other features. Only give permissions that are needed for the app's fundamental functioning.

Managing App Permissions After Installation: You may check and alter app permissions even after installing the app. Navigate to your phone's settings menu and select the "Apps & notifications" section. Select the chosen app and check for the "Permissions" section. Here, you can examine the permissions provided to the app and turn them on or off as required. Be careful with cancelling permissions that are important for the app's fundamental operation.

Installing Security Updates: Maintaining a Secure System

Regularly updating security updates for your phone's operating system and applications is crucial for ensuring maximum security. Here's how to remain updated:

System upgrades: Your Motorola Edge 50 Fusion will get alerts when new system upgrades are available. These updates generally contain security fixes that correct vulnerabilities and safeguard your phone from possible exploitation. It's strongly encouraged to download and apply system updates as soon as they become available. You may often commence the update process immediately from the notice or by heading to your phone's settings menu and selecting the "System" or "Software update" section.

App Updates: App updates may also include security patches and bug fixes. The Google Play Store automatically updates applications by default if you have enabled auto-update capability. You may also manually check for app updates by starting the Play Store app, pressing on your profile icon, choosing "Manage apps & device," and then scrolling to the "Manage" page. This area shows a list of your installed applications, and you may touch on an app to check whether an update is available.

Additional Security Tips for Everyday Use

Here are some extra security steps to consider for regular use:

Download Apps Only from Trusted Sources: The Google Play Store provides a pretty secure environment for downloading apps. However, it's always advisable to use care. Avoid downloading programmes from unknown websites or third-party app shops, since they can include malware or other security threats.

Beware of Phishing Links and Websites: Phishing scams seek to fool you into exposing personal information or clicking on dangerous links. Be careful of emails, text messages, or social media postings that push you to click on strange links or download files from unknown senders.

Use Strong Passwords for Online Accounts: Create strong and unique passwords for your online accounts, including email, social networking, and banking applications. Avoid using the same password for numerous accounts. Consider using a password manager to create and store strong passwords securely.

Enable Two-Factor Authentication (2FA) (Optional): Many online services provide two-factor authentication (2FA) as an extra security layer. 2FA involves an extra verification step beyond your password when login into an account, generally a code given to your phone via text message or created by an authentication app. Enabling 2FA substantially strengthens the security of your online accounts.

Be Wary of Public Wi-Fi: Public Wi-Fi networks might be exposed to eavesdropping. Avoid accessing sensitive information like online banking or financial accounts when connecting to public Wi-Fi. Consider utilising a virtual private network

(VPN) for enhanced protection while accessing public Wi-Fi networks.

By adopting screen lock and password protection, applying fingerprint or face recognition (if applicable), knowing app permissions, and downloading security updates periodically, you've set a good foundation for defending your Motorola Edge 50 Fusion. Remember to be cautious and use care while installing applications, clicking on links, and utilising public Wi-Fi. The next chapter will dig into the intriguing world of the Google Play Store, taking you through exploring its large app library and maximizing your phone's potential.

CHAPTER 10

Advanced Features and Tips for Mastering Your Motorola Edge 50 Fusion

Your Motorola Edge 50 Fusion provides a variety of capabilities beyond basic functionality. This chapter discusses some advanced features and useful hints to unleash the full potential of your phone and tailor your user experience.

Harnessing the Power of Google Assistant

Google Assistant, your built-in virtual assistant, is at your beck and call. Here's how to connect with Google Assistant:

Activating Google Assistant: There are two major methods to activate Google Assistant:

Voice Activation: If your phone enables voice activation (check your settings), you may simply speak the wake word "Hey Google" or "Ok Google" followed by your request.

Assistant Button: Some Motorola Edge 50 Fusion versions include a dedicated Assistant button on the side of the phone. Pressing this button will start Google Assistant, ready to hear your voice requests.

Issuing Voice Commands: Once Google Assistant is engaged, voice your request clearly. You may ask Google Assistant to execute numerous activities, such as:

Setting reminders and alarms
Making calls and sending text messages (hands-free)

Playing music and videos

Searching the web Opening specific applications

Getting weather updates or news briefings

Controlling smart home gadgets (if compatible)

investigating Assistant Settings: Dive further into Google Assistant's capabilities by investigating its settings. You can tweak the wake word, alter response settings, and even build up routines for Google Assistant to conduct certain activities depending on your voice requests.

Capturing the Moment: Screenshots and Screen Recordings

Your Motorola Edge 50 Fusion enables you to capture what's occurring on your screen in two ways: snapshots and screen recordings.

Taking Screenshots: The procedure for getting screenshots could vary somewhat based on your individual model. Here are two popular methods:

Button Combination: Most Motorola Edge 50 Fusion models employ a combination of the power button and volume down button pushed simultaneously to snap a screenshot. Hold both buttons momentarily until you hear a shutter sound or see a screen flash, indicating a successful screenshot capture.

Three-Finger Swipe (Optional): Some models could include a three-finger swipe down motion on the screen to snap a screenshot. Navigate to your phone's settings menu and select the "Gestures" section to determine whether this function is enabled on your device.

Screen Recording: Capture a video of what's occurring on your screen, including app interactions and games, using the screen recording tool. Access the screen recording option via your notification panel (swipe down from the top of the screen) or quick settings panel (swipe down twice from the top of the screen). press on the screen recording icon to commence recording and press it again to stop. The recorded screencast will be stored to your phone's storage.

Maximizing Productivity: Multitasking with Multiple Apps

Your Motorola Edge 50 Fusion lets you multitask by running and toggling between numerous applications concurrently. Here's how to exploit this functionality:

Split-Screen option: This option splits your screen into two pieces, letting you to see and interact with two applications simultaneously. Launch the first app you wish to use in split-screen mode. Navigate to the recent applications menu (usually accessible by sliding up from the bottom of the screen and holding). Tap on the three-dot menu symbol on the app preview of the first app you wish to use in split-screen mode. Select "Split screen" from the menu. Now, pick the second app you want to show on the opposite half of the screen. You may modify the screen size split between the two applications by dragging the dividing line in the middle.

Picture-in-Picture (PIP) Mode (Optional): Supported programmes may be downsized into a resizable and moveable window that floats on top of other apps. This enables you to continue viewing a movie or utilising a certain app while working on something else. Launch the app you wish to use in PIP mode. Tap on the back button or the home button to minimize the app into a PIP window. You may drag the PIP window around the screen to place it comfortably and alter its size by pinching or spreading your fingers on the window.

Enhancing Accessibility: Built-in Features for Everyone

Your Motorola Edge 50 Fusion provides a number of accessibility options to cater to people with diverse requirements. Here are several examples:

Vision Enhancement: Features like text enlargement, color correction, and high contrast mode help increase the visibility of text and material on the screen.

Hearing Assistance: Enable subtitles for calls and videos, change audio balance, or employ boosted audio for increased hearing clarity.

Touch and Interaction: Features like screen reader, talkback, and on-screen buttons may aid people with dexterity problems.

General Settings: Adjust text sizes, display brightness, and notification noises to tailor your phone's user experience for best comfort.

Exploring Accessibility Settings: The accessibility options on your Motorola Edge 50 Fusion are often gathered in a designated "Accessibility" section within the settings menu. Explore this area to learn the numerous features available and adapt them to fit your specific requirements.

Troubleshooting Common Issues: Resolving Minor Hiccups

Even the most advanced technologies may suffer occasional difficulties. Here's how to solve some typical difficulties you can have with your Motorola Edge 50 Fusion:

Battery Drain: If your phone's battery drains quicker than normal, discover likely reasons. Review your battery consumption statistics from the settings menu to identify which applications are taking the most power. Close superfluous background programmes, adjust screen brightness, and deactivate functions you're not using (like Bluetooth or location services) to optimise battery life.

Wi-Fi Connectivity Issues: Ensure your Wi-Fi is switched on and that you're inputting the right password when connecting to a network. Restart your phone and router to repair probable connection issues. If you're still encountering troubles, forget the Wi-Fi network on your phone and try rejoining.

App Crashes: If an app crashes regularly, consider forcing halting the app or restarting your phone. Update the programme to the newest version from the Google Play Store, since updates typically include issue fixes. If the problem continues, try uninstalling and reinstalling the programme.

Slow Performance: Close any unwanted background programmes that could be wasting resources. Restart your phone to delete temporary files and refresh the system. Ensure you have adequate storage space available, since limited storage might influence performance. Consider uninstalling unnecessary programmes or moving data to a microSD card (if applicable) to free up space.

For More Complex difficulties: If you face difficulties beyond these usual situations, visit your phone's user manual or the Motorola support page for troubleshooting methods or to contact customer care for more help.

By utilizing Google Assistant for voice commands and automation, capturing screenshots and screen recordings, multitasking with multiple apps, exploring accessibility features, and troubleshooting common issues, you've unlocked the advanced functionalities of your Motorola Edge 50 Fusion and personalized your user experience for optimal efficiency and enjoyment. The last chapter of this book will include some closing notes and resources for additional investigation.

Chapter 11: Unveiling Hidden Gems: Exploring Advanced Options and Resources

Congratulations! You've mastered the foundations of your Motorola Edge 50 Fusion and unlocked its potential for communication, entertainment, and productivity. This chapter goes into advanced settings and tools to further tailor your experience and discover the hidden depths of your phone.

Tailoring the Experience: Customizing App Notifications

The steady flood of alerts might be daunting. Your Motorola Edge 50 Fusion lets you to modify notification settings for particular applications, ensuring you get the notifications that matter most. Here's how:

Accessing App Notification Settings: Navigate to your phone's settings menu and select the "Apps & notifications" section. This section will give a list of all your installed applications.

Selecting an App: Tap on the individual app for which you wish to personalise alerts. This will access the app's notification settings panel.

Customizing Notification Options: Within the app's notification settings, you may often adjust several elements of how alerts are presented and delivered. Here are some popular options:

Enable/Disable Notifications: Toggle the switch to turn notifications on or off for the whole app.

Notification Sound & Vibration: Choose a particular notification sound or ringtone for the app, or opt for quiet notifications. You may also activate or disable vibration notifications.

Notification Style: Select how alerts look on your screen. Options could include pop-up alerts, notification icons in the status bar, or showing notifications inside the lock screen.

Show Notification Content: Control whether the notification reveals a preview of the message content or keeps it concealed until you open your phone.

Taking Control of Your Notifications: By changing app notification settings, you may design a notification system that corresponds to your preferences. Minimize distractions by disabling irrelevant notifications while ensuring you get timely alerts for texts, calls, or updates from key applications.

Motorola's Hidden Gems: Exploring Unique Features (if relevant)

Some Motorola Edge 50 Fusion variants could come packed with special features designed by Motorola. Here are some possible instances to examine (check your user manual or phone settings for particular capabilities available on your model):

Moto Actions: These gesture-based shortcuts let you activate certain tasks with fast and intuitive hand motions. For example, a chopping motion can activate the flashlight, while twisting your phone in your hand might start the camera app.

Active Display: This function enables you to examine alerts, time, and date even while your phone's screen is off. A double touch on the screen could wake the phone to show the entire notification or unlock the device.

Quick Launch: Navigate to certain applications or features with a quick tap of the fingerprint sensor (if applicable) even while the phone's screen is locked.

Display Modes: Some models could provide several display modes designed for particular conditions. A reading option can optimize the screen for comfortable reading with warmer tones, while a gaming mode would improve graphics for a more immersive gaming experience.

Explore the settings menu on your Motorola Edge 50 Fusion to discover these unique capabilities and tailor your phone's functionality to fit your tastes.

Capturing Stunning Photos: Advanced Camera Settings

The built-in camera on your Motorola Edge 50 Fusion is capable of producing great images and movies. For photography lovers, the camera app provides several sophisticated settings to unlock your creative potential. Here's a peak into some alternatives you could find:

Shooting Modes: Go beyond the basic auto mode and discover additional shooting modes including portrait mode for capturing gorgeous bokeh effects, night mode for low-light photography, or pro mode for finer control over camera settings.

Exposure Controls: Adjust exposure settings like ISO (sensitivity to light) and shutter speed to regulate brightness and capture effects like motion blur or light trails.

White Balance: Fine-tune the white balance to obtain natural-looking colors under diverse lighting situations.

Focus Options: Experiment with manual focus for exact control over where you want the camera to concentrate, or apply spot metering to regulate the exposure for a particular region of the picture.

Resolution and Aspect Ratio: Choose the appropriate resolution for your images, altering image quality and file size. You could also be able to pick the aspect ratio, such as the normal 4:3 or the bigger 16:9 format.

HDR (High Dynamic Range): Enable HDR mode to take shots with a broader range of light and dark details, resulting in more balanced and visually pleasing images.

By studying these advanced camera settings, you may experiment with various approaches and take breathtaking photographs that represent your creative vision. Consult your phone's user manual or other resources for thorough descriptions of each option and how to use them efficiently.

Finding the Help You Need: Resources and Support

Even the most tech-savvy individuals experience occasional obstacles. Here are some useful websites to fix difficulties or enhance your knowledge about your Motorola Edge 50 Fusion:

User Manual and Online Help: Your phone likely comes with a printed user manual or gives access to an online user guide. Refer to these resources for thorough information on utilising different features and fixing common difficulties.

Motorola Support Website: The Motorola support website includes a lot of information, including user manuals, troubleshooting instructions, FAQs, and access to support forums. You may search for particular difficulties or explore related categories to discover solutions.

Google Play Store Help Center: The Google Play Store Help Center provides information and troubleshooting suggestions for applications downloaded from the Play Store. If you're facing troubles with a certain app, this can be a great resource.

Online Communities and Forums: Numerous online communities and forums devoted to Motorola phones exist. These platforms enable you to interact with other users, exchange experiences, ask questions, and discover answers to common issues.

YouTube Tutorials: YouTube provides a wide collection of video tutorials covering different elements of operating your Motorola Edge 50 Fusion. Search for particular subjects or explore channels devoted to tech lessons to obtain useful visual guidance.

By accessing these tools, you may continue learning about your phone's capabilities, solve any difficulties you find, and remain current on the newest software upgrades and features.

The Journey Continues

This tutorial has prepared you with the knowledge and abilities to manage your Motorola Edge 50 Fusion with confidence. As you continue exploring your phone, you'll find even more ways to tailor your experience and harness its capabilities to better your everyday life. Don't hesitate to experiment, explore alternative applications and settings, and seek out extra resources to unlock the full potential of your Motorola Edge 50 Fusion. The world of technology is continually growing, and your phone is a portal to unlimited possibilities. Enjoy the path of discovery.

CONCLUSION

Congratulations! You've reached the last chapter of our detailed guide to mastering your Motorola Edge 50 Fusion. Throughout this voyage, you've examined the main elements, unlocked its functions, and learned tips and methods to maximise your user experience. This last chapter serves as an overview of your learned information and identifies helpful resources for additional investigation.

A Recap of Your Powerful Companion: Key Features and Benefits

The Motorola Edge 50 Fusion delivers a fascinating blend of features intended to improve your mobile experience. Here's a short refresher of some crucial highlights:

Communication Hub: Stay connected with loved ones with clear phone conversations, text messaging, and video chats. Explore messaging applications and social media channels to increase your communication network.

Entertainment on Demand: Immerse yourself with movies, music, games, and eBooks. The bright display and strong processing provide a great entertainment experience.

Photography Powerhouse: Capture amazing photographs and movies with the built-in camera. Explore multiple shooting modes and sophisticated settings to unlock your creative potential.

Productivity Partner: Utilize the calendar app to manage your schedule, make to-do lists, and take notes using the built-in Notes app. Explore a huge array of productivity applications in the Google Play Store to optimise your routine.

Secure and Personalized: Implement screen lock and password security to preserve your info. Customize notification settings and discover accessibility options to tailor your phone for best comfort and security.

Advanced Functionalities: Unlock the hidden jewels supplied by Motorola's unique features (if applicable). Explore sophisticated camera settings for photography aficionados and utilise Google Assistant for voice requests and automation.

This is only a glimpse of the possibilities your Motorola Edge 50 Fusion possesses. As you continue exploring its potential, you'll find even more ways to exploit its features and tailor your experience.

Final Thoughts and Resources for Continued Learning

The world of technology is continually growing, and your Motorola Edge 50 Fusion serves as a portal to discover its unlimited potential. Here are some last ideas and resources to keep you on your learning journey:

Embrace Experimentation: Don't be hesitant to explore with various features, settings, and applications. The simple UI of your Motorola Edge 50 Fusion makes discovery a smooth experience.

Personalize Your Experience: There's no one-size-fits-all strategy to utilising your phone. Customize settings, explore multiple launchers and themes, and build a user experience that corresponds to your tastes.

The Power of applications: The Google Play Store provides a wide library of applications catering to practically every need and interest. Explore various categories, read reviews, and find applications that boost your work, entertainment, or communication.

Stay Updated: Software updates typically include bug fixes, security patches, and even new features. Enable automatic updates whenever feasible to guarantee your phone stays optimal and safe.

Continuous Learning: The materials you studied throughout this course - the user manual, online support websites, forums, and YouTube lessons – are important tools for further learning. Refer to these anytime you meet issues or desire to dive further into certain functions.

The Journey Ahead

The adventure with the Motorola Edge 50 Fusion has just started. With the information obtained from this book and the extensive resources accessible at your fingertips, you have the skills to unlock the full potential of your phone and make it an important companion in your everyday life. Embrace the discovery, tailor your experience, and continue exploring the fascinating possibilities that your Motorola Edge 50 Fusion provides.

As you push forward, realise that the digital world is ever-changing. New applications arise continuously, software upgrades provide new features and enhancements, and the internet community flourishes with useful tips and techniques. Here are some strategies to keep ahead of the curve:

Follow Tech Blogs and Websites: Subscribe to credible tech blogs and websites that specialise on Android smartphones or Motorola devices particularly. These portals include informative evaluations, news about future features, and in-depth tips on using different capabilities.

Connect with the Android Community: Online forums devoted to Android and Motorola phones are active areas for knowledge sharing. Join conversations, ask questions, and learn from the experiences of other users. You could even uncover hidden treasures or unique applications for your phone that you hadn't considered before.

Explore Social Media: Follow Motorola's official social media channels for information about new software upgrades, intriguing features, and useful suggestions. Additionally, try joining social media groups devoted to photography, mobile gaming, or other areas of interest relevant to your phone use. These communities may be a source of inspiration, lessons, and debates about utilising your Motorola Edge 50 Fusion to its best potential.

Remember, the secret to mastering your phone rests in ongoing research and a desire to learn. Don't hesitate to explore, seek out new materials, and ask questions. As you go deeper and tailor your experience, your Motorola Edge 50 Fusion will evolve from a basic gadget into a powerful tool that allows you to remain connected, be productive, and explore the ever-expanding world of mobile technology.

This ends your detailed guide to learning the Motorola Edge 50 Fusion. With the information you've received and the tools at your disposal, you're well on your way to unlocking the full potential of your phone and making it an integral part of your digital life. Happy exploring!

APPENDIX

Understanding your phone's technical characteristics supplies you with useful information about its capabilities and limits. This appendix includes a thorough overview of the Motorola Edge 50 Fusion's basic hardware components, revealing insights into its performance potential.

Network and Connectivity

Cellular Networks: The Motorola Edge 50 Fusion supports several cellular network technologies, letting you to connect to mobile data services from your carrier. Here's a breakdown of the usual network bands supported:

5G NR: Sub-6 GHz (bands may vary based on carrier and model)

4G LTE: FDD-LTE and TD-LTE bands (particular bands supported may vary based on network and device)

3G UMTS

Wi-Fi: The phone supports Wi-Fi protocols 802.11 a/b/g/n/ac/ax, enabling connection to wireless networks for internet access and data transmission.

Bluetooth: The Motorola Edge 50 Fusion has Bluetooth 5.x (precise version may vary depending on model) for wireless connectivity with other Bluetooth-enabled devices like as headphones, speakers, and smartwatches.

NFC (Near Field Communication): This technology allows contactless payments, data interchange with other NFC-equipped devices, and pairing with specific peripherals.

GPS & Navigation: The phone incorporates GPS (Global Positioning System) technology for location services, enabling you to run navigation applications and access location-based functions.

Display

Display Type: The Motorola Edge 50 Fusion has a pOLED (plastic organic light-emitting diode) display, noted for its bright colors, deep blacks, and good viewing angles.

Screen Size: The display measures diagonally, often ranging from 6.6 to 6.8 inches (precise size may vary somewhat depending on model).

Resolution: The display resolution impacts the sharpness and clarity of images. The Motorola Edge 50 Fusion normally features a Full HD+ resolution (2400 x 1080 pixels).

Refresh Rate: The refresh rate refers to the number of times the display refreshes the picture per second. A higher refresh rate (usually 90Hz or 144Hz on the Edge 50 Fusion) gives better images, particularly evident in fast-paced content like gaming or scrolling.

Touchscreen: The display incorporates a capacitive touchscreen enabling easy interaction with the phone's UI.

Processor and Performance

Central Processing Unit (CPU): The CPU is the brain of the phone, responsible for processing data and commands. The Motorola Edge 50 Fusion commonly employs a Qualcomm Snapdragon CPU from the 7 series (particular model may vary based on version).

Number of Cores: The CPU includes numerous cores that conduct tasks concurrently, influencing total performance. The Motorola Edge 50 Fusion likely contains an octa-core CPU (eight cores) for efficient multitasking.

RAM (Random Access Memory): RAM offers temporary storage for running programmes and processes. The Motorola Edge 50 Fusion normally comes with 8GB or 12GB of RAM, providing seamless performance while running numerous programmes concurrently.

Storage

Internal Storage: The phone has internal storage to hold applications, data, photographs, movies, and other stuff. The Motorola Edge 50 Fusion normally comes with 128GB of internal storage, with certain variants having larger capacities.

MicroSD Card Slot (Optional): Some variants of the Motorola Edge 50 Fusion can offer a microSD card slot for extra storage. This enables you to enhance the storage capacity by adding a suitable microSD card (available separately) to store extra data.

Camera

Back Camera System: The Motorola Edge 50 Fusion sports a back camera system with various lenses for recording images and movies. The particular configuration may vary based on the model, however here's a broad breakdown:

Main Sensor: This is the main camera sensor with the greatest resolution, often ranging from 48MP to 50MP.

Ultra-Wide Sensor: This sensor records a broader field of vision than the primary sensor, perfect for shooting landscapes or group shots.

Macro Sensor: This sensor enables you to shoot close-up photos with a high degree of clarity.

Additional Sensors (Optional): Some models could contain additional sensors for functions like depth sensing or telephoto zoom.

Front Camera: The front-facing camera is utilised for selfies, video calls, and face recognition. The resolution of the front camera normally varies from 16MP to 32MP depending on the model.

Camera options: The camera app provides numerous options to improve your picture experience. These can include HDR mode for taking photographs with a broader range of light and dark details, night mode for low-light photography, portrait mode for capturing bokeh effects, and numerous shooting modes like panoramic or slow motion.

Battery

Battery Capacity: The battery capacity is measured in milliampere-hours (mAh) and reflects the phone's possible battery life. The Motorola Edge 50 Fusion often has a big battery, sometimes ranging from 4,800mAh to 5,000mAh, providing longer usage on a single charge.

Fast Charging: The phone features fast charging technology, enabling you to swiftly refresh the battery level. The particular fast charging technology supported (e.g., Motorola TurboPower) will differ based on the model.

Operating System

Operating System: The Motorola Edge 50 Fusion runs the Android operating system, possibly the newest version of Android (at the time of introduction) with Motorola's proprietary user interface on top. This user interface could provide more features and modifications compared to vanilla Android.

Software

Pre-installed applications: The phone comes pre-installed with a selection of critical applications from Google and Motorola. These could include Gmail, Chrome, YouTube, Camera, Photos, Calendar, and other productivity or leisure applications. You may also download more applications from the Google Play Store.

Physical Dimensions and Weight

measurements: The physical measurements of the phone are normally measured in millimetres (mm) and indicate its height, breadth, and thickness. The Motorola Edge 50 Fusion is likely a compact and lightweight phone, making it pleasant to grip and carry.

Weight: The weight of the phone is measured in grams (g) and might vary based on the materials used in its production. The Motorola Edge 50 Fusion is likely meant to be lightweight and portable.

Materials

Frame: The frame of the phone offers structural support and may be manufactured from different materials like plastic or metal.

Back Panel: The back panel of the phone may be built from various materials including plastic, glass, or a mix of both.

Sensors

Fingerprint Sensor (Optional): Some variants of the Motorola Edge 50 Fusion can contain a fingerprint sensor incorporated in the display or positioned on the back panel for safe unlocking of the phone.

Other Sensors: The phone could incorporate other sensors such an accelerometer, gyroscope, magnetometer, proximity sensor, and ambient light sensor to allow other capabilities.

www.ingramcontent.com/pod-product-compliance
Lightning Source LLC
Chambersburg PA
CBHW050100230526
45470CB00004B/1610